English Explained 5:
The Future Tenses

ESL Made Easy with
The Be/Have/(Do) Grammar Matrix™

By John C Lipes

BERKSHIRE SCHOOL OF ENGLISH
Email: info@berkshireschoolofenglish.co.uk
Telephone: 01635 45900
www.berkshireschoolofenglish.co.uk

A New and Easy Way to Learn English:
The Be/Have/(Do) Grammar Matrix™

How to Think in English: Be Something! Have Something! Do Something!

Acknowledgments

A huge Thank You to the schools that allowed me to develop and test the Be/Have/(Do) Methodology.

If you are able to attend any of these reputable institutions, I highly recommend them all:

Southern States University
www.ssu.edu

The International Academy of English
www.sdiae.edu

The University of California San Diego
www.ucsd.edu

Human International Academy
www.hiausa.com

Sprachcafé Düsseldorf
www.sprachcaffe-duesseldorf.de

Hamburg School of English
www.hamburg.school-of-english.de

YES: Your English School Hamburg
www.yes-school.de

Berlitz Language Schools Germany
www.berlitz.com

Photos by Kjel Nassau
www.bedandbay.com

Clip Art from
www.ace-clipart.com
www.freepic.com
www.sweetclipart.com
www.freeclipartnow.com

Crazy Culture Tip, pg. 45
www.informationcentral0.tripod.com

Table of Contents

The Be/Have/(Do) Grammar Matrix™

	Be Simple and Progressive	Have Simple	(Do) Simple
Present	am am (doing) is is (doing) are are (doing)	have has	(do) (does)
Present Perfect	have been have been (doing) has been has been (doing)	have had has had	have (done) has (done)
Past	was was (doing) were were (doing)	had	(did)
Past Perfect	had been had been (doing)	had had	had (done)
Future	will be will be (doing)	will have	will (do)
Future Perfect	will have been will have been (doing)	will have had	will have (done)

The entire language can be seen in the Be/Have/(Do) Grammar Matrix™

How Can I Think in English?

This series of books explains English like no other books you have ever seen.

The key to thinking in English is to recognize the patterns that we use. We have a very simple structure in English: Subject + Verb + Object (SVO). These can be seen as 'chunks' of information.

This book will show you how to think in English by showing you language patterns on a very simple chart called the Be/Have/(Do) Grammar Matrix.

What is the Be/Have/(Do) Methodology?

The entire English language can be identified in the Be/Have/(Do) Grammar Matrix:

In order to communicate in any language, you have to express things that describe what you are, what you have, and what you do. There are so many different languages in the world, but all languages have this in common.

The Be/Have/(Do) Methodology was developed to demonstrate the various grammar forms in English in an easy-to-understand comprehensive format.

Dividing the language into these three areas will make it easy to identify the different language functions and understand how they are used.

This format will clearly show the differences between the Simple Forms and the Progressive Forms, as well as the Perfect Forms.

Notice that (doing) is the Progressive Form and is always under the Be Column.

(do / does), (did), and (done) are the Simple Forms and are always under the (Do) Column.

Be Something!
Be (Doing) Something!
Have Something!
Do Something!

	Be Simple and Progressive Forms	Have Simple Form Only	(Do) Simple Form Only
Present 1st Verb	am am (doing) is is (doing) are are (doing)	have has	(do) (does)
Present Perfect 3rd Verb	have been have been (doing) has been has been (doing)	have had has had	have (done) has (done)
Past 2nd Verb	was was (doing) were were (doing)	had	(did)
Past Perfect 3rd Verb	had been had been (doing)	had had	had (done)
Future 1st Verb	will be will be (doing)	will have	will (do)
Future Perfect 3rd Verb	will have been will have been (doing)	will have had	will have (done)

Understanding the Be/Have/(Do) Grammar Matrix:

You can **be** something or you can **be (doing)** something, you can **have** something, or you can **(do)** something.

These four concepts entirely encompass the English language and can be expressed in three columns representing Be Verbs, Have Verbs, and (Do) Verbs.

All languages have this ideology in common and base their 'thinking' on the three concepts of being something, having something, and doing something.

In English, we also have two special forms. The Progressive, which describes actions that are happening at the time being spoken about, a Perfect Form, which ties the concepts of the Present with the Past in the Present Perfect; a point of time in the past with a time span before that with the Past Perfect, and a point of time in the future and a time span before that in the Future Perfect.

The Progressive Form is always found with a Be Verb; the Simple Form has a Be Verb, a Have Verb, and a (Do) Verb. These are the 'bones' or 'skeleton' on which English is built.

Why are there parentheses around the (Do) Verbs?

Sometimes, we use the word, do, as the Main Verb, but often, we replace it with another Main Verb. (Do) Verbs can be expressed in the Simple Tense or the Progressive Tense.

Simple: There is no difference between the following sentences, which express something that happens regularly, and they are found under the (Do) Column:

I **do** yoga.	**(do)** something
I **practice** yoga.	**(do)** something

Progressive: If we want to express the active nature of something, or to show that it is unusual or temporary, we use the Be Verb followed by a (Do) Verb in the Progressive Form. The (Do) Verb is always represented in the Present Progressive. The Be Verb always comes first and changes according to tense, which is why this form is found under the Be Column:

I **am doing** yoga.	**be (doing)** something
I **was practicing** yoga.	**be (doing)** something

English is full of exceptions and has elements from many different languages. Using the Be/Have/(Do) Grammar Matrix will help you understand how to look at the parts or chunks of a sentence to identify the meaning or function of a word.

For example, we use the word, **have**, as an indicator of the Perfect Tense. We don't think of it literally as, **have**, but rather as an indicator of a chunk of the sentence that belongs to a structure; *have* been something, *have* been (doing) something, *have* had something, *have* (done) something, etc.

The same is true of the combination, **going to**, which means, **will**, NOT (doing) to. **Have to**, and, **has to**, mean, **must**!

We will examine all forms in-depth in this book.

Learning how to see the parts of a sentence will help you master the language much quicker.

English is based on simple structures and repeating patterns that intertwine.

Understanding Be

You can **be** something or you can **be (doing)** something.

We use the language functions under the Be Column to express both the Simple Form as well as the Progressive Form. Recognizing this will help you understand and speak English much better.

The Progressive Form always starts with the Subject followed by a Be Verb (I am), followed by a (Do) Verb in the Progressive Form (teaching).

For things that are always true or happen regularly, or for describing our state-of-being, we use the Present Simple under the Be Column:

I **am** American.   Always
I **am** a teacher.   Regularly
I **am** happy.   State-of-being

We also use the Present Tense for the future. There is no difference between the following sentences:

I **am** a delegate at the next convention.
I **will be** a delegate at the next convention.
I **am going to be** a delegate at the next convention.

Remember, **am going to**, means, **will**. It is a Simple Form, NOT a Progressive Form.

When we speak about things that are happening right now or around now, or at the time the speaker is specifically identifying, we use the Progressive Forms under the Be Column:

I **am teaching** grammar.		Be (doing)
I **will be teaching** grammar.		Be (doing)
I **am going to be teaching** grammar.		Be (doing)

Important Note about the Progressive and other -ing Forms:

The Progressive -ing Forms are always found in the Be Column to show action at that time, but many English words end with -ing. The same is true of the ending, -ed, which is not always an indicator of the past. The placement of the word determines what it means. That is why it is important to see the language in chunks. We will examine these forms throughout this series of books.

Understanding Have

The Have Column describes things that we possess or own:

I	**have**	a textbook.	Tangible
I	**have**	a dream.	Intangible

Important note on the word, **have**, and the Perfect Forms: we use the word, **have**, to identify the Perfect Form, but notice that it is used differently or in addition to the Main Verb, **have**.

We will examine this form in-depth in Single Lesson Four: The Present Perfect, Single Lesson Five: The Past Perfect, and Single Lesson Seven: The Future Perfect.

The following sentence belongs in the Be Column. The word, **have**, only indicates the Present Perfect. I was in the past and I still am this now:

I	**have been**	a surfer for 16 years.

The following sentence belongs in the Have Column. The word, **have**, only indicates the Present Perfect. I had this in the past and I still have this now:

I	**have had**	a lot of good times.

The following sentence belongs in the (Do) Column. The word, **have**, only indicates the Present Perfect. I (did) this in the past and I still (do) this now:

I	**have (done)**	many tricks on my surfboard.

Why do we use the word, **have**? Because the Perfect Form is used to indicate three concepts involving experiences that we possess in our life-experience:

1. We have this truth in our lives and it is relevant now, even though it happened in the past. (Present Perfect)

2. We had this truth in the past from a certain point until another point in the past and it was relevant to the time being talked about in the past. (Past Perfect)

3. It is true now or will be true in the future until a time further in the future and even though it may be happening now, or will be happening in the future, the relevance is placed on the result in the further future, at a point when we will have had this truth in our lives for a certain amount of time. (Future Perfect)

Understanding (Do)

When we speak about things that we always do or things that happen regularly, we use the Simple Forms under the (Do) Column:

| I | **teach** | English. |
| He | **teaches** | English. |

He, She, It: add the 's'

Sometimes we use the verb, (**do**), as the Main Verb, but we often replace it with another Verb. That is why the (Do) Verbs are in parentheses in this book.

| I | **do** | my homework | (Do) as the Main Verb |
| I | **read** | my textbook. | (Do) as a different Verb |

The (Do) Verbs have three forms. We use the 1st Verb to talk about the Present Tense and the Future Tense (go).

We use the 2nd Verb to talk about the Past Tense (went).

We use the 3rd Verb for all three Perfect Forms: Present Perfect, Past Perfect, and Future Perfect (gone).

We often combine the Be/Have/(Do) Verbs with each other in different forms, which will be discussed in more depth in each chapter.

This often confuses students learning English, but by using the Be/Have/(Do) Grammar Matrix, you will be able to easily identify why certain grammar structures are used and the concepts they convey.

I **am doing** my homework.	**be (doing)**
I **am having** a great time.	**be (doing)**
I **have finished** my homework.	**have (done)**
Do you **have** homework?	**(do) have**

What **have** you **been doing** lately? **have been (doing)**

English is also a language that incorporates words and phrases from many languages, so there are many exceptions found in grammar and vocabulary, which will be examined more closely in the various chapters.

When you learn new words, identify them on the Be/Have/(Do) Grammar Matrix and make notes in your notebook.

I	**am**	a teacher.	**be**
I	**am teaching**	English.	**be (doing)**
I	**have**	students.	**have**
I	**teach**	English.	**(do)**

What are you?

What are you doing?

What do you have?

What do you do?

The past, the present, and the future went into a bar…

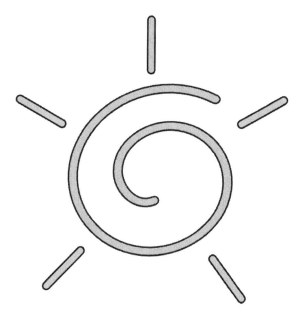

It was tense!

Get the Most out of these Books!

Start by reading the Introduction about Understanding the Be/Have/(Do) Grammar Matrix.

As you read new words throughout this series, learn them as Be Verbs, Have Verbs, or Do Verbs.

Be: To be extraordinary
Have: To have manners
Do: To edify

This will allow you to learn the language in chunks of information and show you how to think in the English Subject-Verb-Object Structure (SVO).

Pay attention to the patterns in the various forms, which repeat themselves in each tense.

Write complete answers, even when the answers are easy. This action will help you retain the language and remember the patterns much easier. Don't rush. Think about the examples.

This series of books will also teach you the difference between Academic English and Everyday Spoken English. Read the Appendices-they are full of fun facts as well as vital information.

When learning the Basic Building Blocks, you will learn basic structures showing you the placement of Verbs, Nouns, and Adjectives. Learn about Adverbs in Single Lesson Nine: Adverbs.

Pay attention to the **S**ubject, which can be one word or a chunk of information.

Pay attention to the **V**erb, which can be one word or a long combination of words.

Pay attention to the **O**bject, which can be one word or a chunk of information, just like the Subject.

If a chunk of information does not make sense on its own it is called a Phrase.

If a chunk of information has its own Subject-Verb-Object combination, it is called a Clause.

Subject + Verb + Object = SVO

I + love + you.
Single Words

The two books + have been + fun to write.
Phrases

The books I wrote + are going to help + you learn easily.
Clauses

When you learn about a new topic, make notes on what that topic can be, what it can have, and what it can do. This will vastly increase your ability to talk about the topic and express yourself more clearly.

Have fun!

Be Sure to Get All the Books in This Series!

Single Lessons:	**The Appendices**
Single Lesson One:	**The Present Tenses**
Single Lesson Two:	**The Past Tenses**
Single Lesson Three:	**The Present Perfect**
Single Lesson Four:	**The Past Perfect**
Single Lesson Five:	**The Future Tenses**
Single Lesson Six:	**The Future Perfect**
Single Lesson Seven:	**The Verbs**
Single Lesson Eight:	**The Adverbs**
Single Lesson Nine:	**The Clauses**
Single Lesson Ten:	**The Verbals**
Single Lesson Eleven:	**Reported Speech**
Single Lesson Twelve:	**The Conditionals**
Single Lesson Fourteen:	**Nouns and Adjectives**

Think about the Future. What do you want to be? What do you want to be doing at a certain point in the future? What do you want to have? What do you want to do?

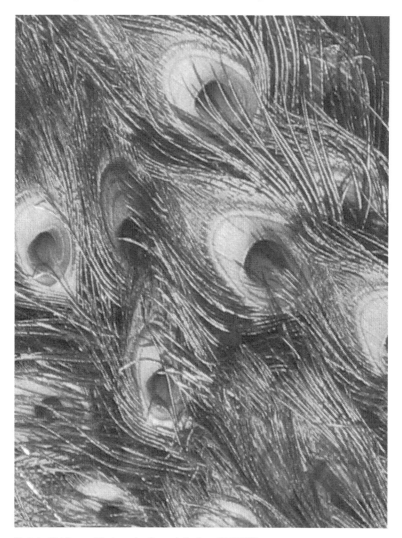

Photo by Kjel Nassau iPhotography, Peacock Feathers CA © 2006

Single Lesson Five

The Future
'Then - When'

"To practice **five** things under all circumstances constitutes perfect virtue; these **five** are
gravity, generosity of soul, sincerity, earnestness, and kindness."
Confucius

Chapter Vocabulary

to constitute	to be spontaneous	the Euro zone
to be kind	the front row	to be earnest
to succeed	to have a goal	to be pretty sure
to go crazy	circumstances	to be inconvenienced
to graduate	to have virtue	an aunt
to get accepted to university	gravity	an uncle
to race	to be generous	a sports car
to date	to be sincere	a photo shoot
to BBQ	to have supper	a projector
to sneeze	a tissue	a waiter

Learning Goal

Grammar Presentation 1: The Future Tenses

Grammar Presentation 2: Positive and Negative Contractions

Grammar Presentation 3: Basic Building Blocks

Grammar Presentation 4: The Present Tense for the Future

Grammar Presentation 5: Asking Basic Questions

Grammar Presentation 6: Short Answers

Grammar Presentation 7: The 5W's and How Questions

Grammar Presentation 8: Future Emphatic

In a Nutshell

Future	Be	Have	(Do)
Future Simple	will be going to be	will have going to have	will (do) going to (do)
Future Progressive	will be (doing) going to be (doing)		

Future Will:

I / You / We / They / He / She / It + Will + Be/Have/(Do) + Something = SVO

I	will be	at the premiere.	Be
You	will be	at the after-party.	Be
We	will be dancing	all night long.	Be (doing)
They	will be playing	our song.	Be (doing)
He	will have	a great time.	Have
She	will serve	a large buffet.	(Do)
It	will have	fresh seafood.	Have

Future Going To:

Remember that this form looks like a Progressive Verb, but means, **will**, NOT: (**doing**) **to**. That means that you will sometimes hear the words, **going to**, to mean, **will**, followed by, **go**, or, **be going**, as the Verb and then followed by a

Prepositional Phrase that starts with the word, **to**. Thus, you could get the following sentences:

I   will go   to Argentina soon.
         (Do)

I   am going to go   to Argentina soon.
         (Do)

I   am going to be going to Argentina soon.
         Be (doing)

Of course, in English, we like to keep it short and simple, so the last form sounds really wordy. Most people would choose the Will Form when the Verb is, **go**.

Likewise, to will something, means to wish something. If we use the word, **will**, as a Verb, then we normally choose the Going To Form:

I   will will   a great future.
         (Do)

I   am going to will   a great future.
         (Do)

Because of its form, **going to**, is always found in combination with a Be Verb.

I + Am Going To + Be/Have/(Do) + Something?

I   am going to be   a best-selling author!
         Be

He / She / It + Is Going To + Be/Have/(Do) + Something?

He   is going to be   Prime Minister!
         Be

She   is going to be   a superstar!
         Be

| It | is going to be
Be | a magnificent year! |

You / We / They + Are Going To + Be/Have/(Do) + Something?

You	are going to master (Do)	the English language!
We	are going to work (Do)	together online!
They	are going to give (Do)	my book great reviews!

Thinking in English

Future Tense	Be	Have	(Do)
Both Forms are often interchangeable, but we use the Will Form for Spontaneous situations and we use the Going To Form for Planned situations.	will be something. OR am going to be something. will be (doing) something. OR am going to be (doing) something. will be something. OR is going to be something. will be (doing) something. OR is going to be (doing) something. will be something. OR are going to be something. will be (doing) something. OR are going to be (doing) something.	will have something. OR am going to have something. will have something. OR is going to have something. will have something. OR are going to have something.	will (do) something. OR am going to (do) something. will (do) something. OR is going to (do) something. will (do) something. OR are going to (do) something.

You will be something!

I
am going to be / will be
something.

He / She / It
is going to be / will be
something.

You / We / They
are going to be / will be
something.

You will be (doing) something!

I
am going to be (doing) / will be (doing)
something.

He / She / It
is going to be (doing) / will be (doing)
something.

You / We / They
are going to be (doing) / will be (doing)
something.

You will have something!

I
am going to have / will have
something.

He / She / It
is going to have / will have
something.

You / We / They
are going to have / will have
something.

You will (do) something!

I
am going to (do) / will (do)
something.

He / She / It
is going to (do) / will (do)
something.

You / We / They
are going to (do) / will (do)
something.

In the Future Tense, you **will be** something or you **will be (doing)** something, you **will have** something, or you **will (do)** something.

You will notice that there are two basic forms, **Will**, and, **Going To**. The Going To Forms are just as common as the Will Forms and the two are used in different ways.

We have three different forms for the future. You can say, **will**, or, **going to**, to talk about the future.

I   **will**   graduate.
        (Do)

I   **am going to**   graduate.
        (Do)

We can also use the Present Tense for the Future by making a Present Tense sentence and adding the Time Indicator:

I   **am graduating**   next month.
        Be (doing)

I will be something!
I will be (doing) something!
I will have something!
I will (do) something!

In-Depth Analysis

The Future: Will and Going To

The Future Form with, **going to,** is another example of the Be/Have/(Do) Verbs crossing functions.

Remember, the Have Verb in the Perfect Forms should only be understood as an indicator of the Perfect Form rather than meaning, **have**. The Future Form has an example that is similar. The word combination, **going to**, also needs to be seen as a simple indicator of the Future Form and not as, (**doing**) **to**. The word combination means, **will**, but we use it to distinguish whether what we are talking about is planned or not. There are many exceptions; it just depends on what you are talking about.

We don't have specific contractions for, **going to,** in proper English, but as anyone knows from media and entertainment, we tend to shorten forms, especially in spoken English. This is where the term, **gonna,** comes from. While **gonna** is not a proper word, rather a slang hybrid meaning, **going to**, it is universally common and needs to be understood. The slang word, **wanna**, is also very common and means, **want to**.

Neither of these words should ever be written in academic or proper English, but are perfectly acceptable pronunciation when speaking.

I'm **gonna** order a book.   I am **going to** order a book.
Will (Do)

I **wanna** be a rock star.   I **want to** be a rock star.
(Do)

A common mistake with the future is to use the wrong form with Time Clauses. When speaking about the future in combination with a time clause, the verb reverts to the Present Simple:

When the concert **starts**, I **will be** in the front row.
Be

NOT: When the concert will start, I will be in the front row.

When we offer to do things, the form we use depends on the situation. **Will**, is used for such things as volunteering to do something and we use contractions to make it sound casual:

I'll pick you up in the morning.   (Do)

In order to sound more firm, we use, **going to,** which can't be contracted.

I **am going to** pick you up in the morning.   (Do)

Here the speaker sounds like he has made a decision and will do something for a specific purpose. Perhaps the listener does not want the speaker to be inconvenienced, but the speaker is insisting because of some reason. Perhaps it is going to snow.

To make it sound more casual, the speaker could say, **gonna**, with a contraction:

I'm **gonna** pick you up in the morning.   (Do)

We also tend to use **will** to announce things, even if they were planned in advance:

We **will have** a test next week.   Have

We **will be** in Miami at 1:30pm.   Be

We **will have** supper at 8pm.   Have

We **will meet** in the lobby at 9am.   (Do)

After the announcement has been made, the Going To Form is usually used to discuss it.

A: What are we doing tomorrow?
B: We are **going to meet** in the lobby at 9am.

If you make predictions about the future, you can use, **will**, or, **going to**:

What **will** the future **be** like?   Be

What **is** the future **going to be** like?	Be (doing)
What **will** you **be doing** in five years?	Be (doing)
What **are** you **going to be doing** in five years?	Be (doing)
What **will** the next smart phones **have**?	Have
What **are** the new phones **going to have**?	Have
Where **will** humans **live** in 100 years?	(Do)
Where **are** humans **going to live** in 100 years?	(Do)

We also use the Present Tense for future times. This is very common, especially in spoken English. All of the following sentences mean the same thing:

I will go to Spain in September.	(Do)
I'll go to Spain in September.	(Do)
I am going to go to Spain in September.	(Do)
I'm going to go to Spain in September.	(Do)

But look at the last sentence. The combination, **going to go**, sounds redundant. In this case, it sounds more natural to use the Present Progressive. The Future is clear from the Time Phrase, **in September**.

I am going to Spain in September.	Be (doing)
I'm going to Spain in September.	Be (doing)

Grammar Presentation 1: The Future Tense

Remember: You can always talk about the future by using a Present Tense Sentence in combination with a Future Time:

Present Tense Sentence:	**Future Time:**
I am working **Be (doing)**	next week.
I have class **Have**	tomorrow.
I speak at the conference **(Do)**	this weekend.

Otherwise, we have two proper Future Forms. We use the Will Form for more spontaneous actions, and we use the Going To Form for things that we have planned. Again, the tone makes the music, the Verbs and other words being used have an impact, and sometimes there is no difference between the forms.

Future Tense Will Positive	Be	Have	(Do)
I / You / We / They / He / She / It	will be something will be (doing) something	will have something	will (do) something

I	will be **Be**	at home.
You	will be **Be**	in Berlin.
We	will be traveling **Be (doing)**	to Napa Valley.
They	will have **Have**	a wine tour.
He	will have **Have**	a glass of wine.
She	will buy **(Do)**	a set of wine glasses.

It   will do   color printing.
       (Do)

Here are the Going To Forms. Remember that they are always in combination with a Be Verb:

Future Tense Going To Positive	Be	Have	(Do)
I	am going to be something am going to be (doing) something	am going to have something	am going to (do) something
He / She / It	is going to be something is going to be (doing) something	is going to have something	is going to (do) something
You / We / They	are going to be something are going to be (doing) something	are going to have something	are going to (do) something

I   am going to be   in London.
       Be

I   am going to be visiting   a museum.
       Be (doing)

I   am going to have   a docent.
       Have

I   am going to visit   the Tate Museum.
       (Do)

He   is going to be   a doctor.
       Be

He   is going to be studying   for a long time.
        Be (doing)

He   is going to have   a lot of classes.
        Have

He   is going to practice   medicine.
        (Do)

You   are going to be   a huge success.
        Be

You   are going to be doing   so much.
        Be (doing)

You   are going to have   a great life.
        Have

You   are you going to do   great things.
        (Do)

Future Tense Will Negative	Be	Have	(Do)
I / You / We / They / He / She / It	**will not be something** **will not be (doing) something**	**will not have something**	**will not (do) something**

I   will not be   at the show.
        Be

You   will not be   bothered.
        Be

We   will not be taking   that course.
        Be (doing)

They   will not be doing   the gig.
        Be (doing)

He   will not have   enough time.
        Have

She	will not have **Have**	any problems.

It	will not decide **(Do)**	now.

Future Tense Going To Negative	Be	Have	(Do)
I	am not going to be something am not going to be (doing) something	am not going to have something	am not going to (do) something
He / She / It	is not going to be something is not going to be (doing) something	is not going to have something	is not going to (do) something
You / We / They	are not going to be something are not going to be (doing) something	are not going to have something	are not going to (do) something

As a general rule, when we have planned something and we are pretty sure it is going to come true, we use the Going To Form. We use the Will Form when speaking spontaneously.

I	am not going to be **Be**	on time.

He	is going to be **Be**	late.

She	is going to be acting **Be (doing)**	in the play.

It	is going to have **Have**	three acts.

You	are going to enjoy **(Do)**	it.
We	are going to buy **(Do)**	tickets.
They	are going to have **Have**	refreshments.

Quick Practice 1: The Future Tense

Choose the correct form:

1. A: Where will you go to college*?
   B: I **will go** / **am going to** go to UCLA. I got accepted last month!

2. A: Where will you go to college?
   B: I'm not sure. I think I **will** / **am going to** spend a year at community college.

3. A: Oops! I dropped my cell phone!
   B: Don't worry, I **will** get / **am going to** get that for you.

4. A: What are you doing this weekend?
   B: I don't know. I think I **will** have / **am going to** have a BBQ.

5. A: What are you doing this weekend?
   B: I **will** have / **am going to** have a BBQ. We planned it last week.

The difference is not always clear, and both forms have situations that make them appropriate. In some cases, however, like in spontaneous decisions, the Will Form is used and the Going To Form sounds unnatural. If somebody sneezes, you would say, "I'll get you a tissue." It would sound strange to say, "I'm going to get you a tissue."

In everyday spoken English however, the tendency is to use the short forms. At a restaurant, it is more common to say, "I'll have a salad," even if that person had made that decision long before they went to the restaurant.

The best advice is to not think about it too much and to use whichever form feels natural at that moment. Also pay attention to how native speakers switch between both forms.

In all of the examples above, there are situations where you might hear either form. Only in the third example is it important to use the will form.

Grammar Presentation 2: Positive and Negative Contractions

Future Contractions	Be	Have	(Do)
I	I'll be I'll not be* **I won't be**	I'll have I'll not have* **I won't have**	I'll (do) I'll not (do)* **I won't (do)**
He	He'll be He'll not be* **He won't be**	He'll have He'll not have* **He won't have**	He'll (do) He'll not (do)* **He won't (do)**
She	She'll be She'll not be* **She won't be**	She'll have She'll not have* **She won't have**	She'll (do) She'll not (do)* **She won't (do)**
It	It'll be It'll not be* **It won't be**	It'll have It'll not have* **It won't have**	It'll (do) It'll not (do)* **It won't (do)**
You	You'll be You'll not be* **You won't be**	You'll have You'll not have* **You won't have**	You'll (do) You'll not (do)* **You won't (do)**
We	We'll be We'll not be* **We won't be**	We'll have We'll not have* **We won't have**	We'll (do) We'll not (do)* **We won't (do)**
They	They'll be They'll not be* **They won't be**	They'll have They'll not have* **They won't have**	They'll (do) They'll not (do)* **They won't (do)**

*Notice that the **–'ll be**, **-'ll have**, and, **-'ll (do)** forms sound very formal.

The most common forms are, **won't be**, **won't have**, and, **won't** (**do**).

We only have Contractions for the Will Form. For the Going To Form, you can Contract the Subject and the Be Verb (I'm / He's / You're, etc.), but the words, **going to**, do not have a Contraction Form:

Quick Practice 2: Positive and Negative Contractions

Think about your future goals and dreams.

What would you be if you could be anything in the world?

Imagine that you could be that person.

All of your dreams will come true in the future.

Write sentences about this 'future you':

1.   My dream job_____ .

Now imagine yourself in the future. Write sentences using contractions:

2.   I will be_____ .

3.   I will not be_____ .

4.   I will be (doing) _____ .

5.   I will not be (doing)_____ .

6.   I will have _____ .

7.   I will not have._____ .

8.   I will (do) _____ .

9.   I will not (do) _____ .

Grammar Presentation 3: Basic Building Blocks

Look at these basic simple constructions for the Going To Form in the familiar SVO structure:

Subject +	Be, Have or (Do) Verb +	Object
I	am going to be am going to be (doing) am going to have am going to (do)	something.
He She It	is going to be is going to be (doing) is going to have is going to (do)	something.
You We They	are going to be are going to be (doing) are going to have are going to be (do)	something.

The Object represents something. This 'something' can come in many forms. In this unit, we will look at some basic verb expressions possible under each of the Be/Have/(Do) Columns.

You **are going to be** something or you **are going to be (doing)** something. Look at these sentences describing the future from the Be Column:

I **am going to be** older.
Subject + Verb + Adjective
Older is something.

I **am going to be** a rock star.
Subject + Verb + Noun
A rock star is something.

I **am going to** be a great uncle.
Subject + Verb + Adjective + Noun
A great uncle is something.

I **am going to be traveling** Europe.
Subject + (doing) + Noun
Europe is something.

You **are going to have** things, so to describe them, you can use a Noun or a combination of Adjective and Noun. Look at these sentences from the Have Column:

I **am going to have** a car.
Subject + Verb + Noun
A car is something.

I **am going to have** a sports car.
Subject + Verb + Adjective + Noun
A sports car is something.

And finally, you are **going to (do)** something. Look at these possibilities:

I **am going to teach**.
Subject + Verb + [Understood]
I am going to teach something.

I **am going to teach** English.
Subject + Verb + Adjective
English is something.

I **am going teach** English grammar.
Subject + Verb + Adjective + Noun
English grammar is something.

Now let's look at the same combinations with will:

Future Tense	Be	Have	(Do)
All Forms	will be + adjective will be + noun will be + adjective + noun will be + (doing)	will have + noun will have + adjective + noun	will (do) will (do) + noun will (do) + adjective + noun

Look at these basic simple constructions for the **will** form in the same SVO Form:

You **will be** something or you **will be (doing)** something. Look at these sentences describing the future from the Be Column:

Will Be

I **will be** older.
Subject + Verb + Adjective
Older is something.

I **will be** a rock star.
Subject + Verb + Noun
A rock star is something.

I **will** be a great uncle.
Subject + Verb + Adjective + Noun
A great uncle is something.

I **will be traveling** Europe.
Subject + (doing) + Noun
Europe is something.

Will Have

You **will have** things, so to describe them, you can use a Noun or a combination of Adjective and Noun. Look at these sentences from the Have Column:

I **will have** a car.
Subject + Verb + Noun
A car is something.

I **will have** a sports car.
Subject + Verb + Adjective + Noun
A sports car is something.

Will (Do)

I **will teach**.
Subject + Verb + [Understood]
I will teach something.

I **will teach** English.
Subject + Verb + Adjective
English is something.

I **will teach** English grammar.
Subject + Verb + Adjective + Noun
English grammar is something.

Quick Practice 3: Basic Building Blocks

Using the chart above, create sentences of your own with the Going To Form:

Subject	Be Verb	Adjective	Noun
I			X
I		X	
I			
Subject	Have Verb	Adjective	Noun
I		X	
I			
Subject	(Do) Verb	Adjective	Noun
I		X	X
I		X	
I			

Using the chart above, create sentences of your own with the Will Form:

Subject	Be Verb	Adjective	Noun
I			X
I		X	
I			

Subject	Have Verb	Adjective	Noun
I		X	
I			
Subject	**(Do) Verb**	**Adjective**	**Noun**
I		X	X
I		X	
I			

Grammar Presentation 4: Present Tense for the Future

In order to make things shorter and easier, we often use the Present Tense in combination with a Future Time Indicator to indicate future actions.

This can be in the immediate future or distant future:

Present Tense for the Future	Subject	Be/Have/(Do) Verb	Object	Future Time Indicator
Be	I	am	a graduate	in 3 weeks.
Be (doing)	I	am doing	my homework	tonight.
Have	I	have	a date	on Saturday.
(Do)	I	graduate	(understood: from school)	in 2017.
Be	He /She / It	is	a parent	next month.
Be (doing)	He / She / It	is buying	toys	tomorrow.

Have	He /She / It	has	a meeting	next month.
(Do)	He /She / It	performs	(understood: the performance)	on Wednesday.
Be	You / We / They	are	in Tokyo	next week.
Be (doing)	You / We / They	are working	(understood: the task)	after lunch.
Have	You / We / They	have	a photo shoot	at 2pm.
(Do)	You / We / They	give	our report	at 11am.

Quick Practice 4: Present Tense for the Future

Think about things that you have already planned.

Using the Present Tense with a Future Time Indicator, complete the following table with sentences of your own.

Check your answers with your teacher:

Present Tense for the Future	Subject	Be/Have/(Do) Verb	Object	Future Time Indicator
Be	I			
Be (doing)	I			
Have	I			
(Do)	I			

Be	He /She / It			
Be (doing)				
Have				
(Do)				
Be	You / We / They			
Be (doing)				
Have				
(Do)				

Grammar Presentation 5: Asking Basic Questions

Will Questions	Be	Have	(Do)
I / You / We / They / He / She / It	Will X be something? Will X be (doing) something?	Will X have something?	Will X (do) something?

Will I   be late?
Be

Will I   be rushing around?
Be (doing)

Will you   have time?
Have

Will we   have lunch?
               Have

Will they   serve salad?
               (Do)

Will he   be OK?
               Be

Will she   be performing?
               Be (doing)

Will it   cost money?
               (Do)

The Going To Form is more varied than the Will Form, but you are already familiar with this pattern.

Going To Questions	Be	Have	(Do)
I	Am I going to be something? Am I going to be (doing) something?	Am I going to have something?	Am I going to (do) something?
He / She / It	Is X going to be something? Is X going to be (doing) something?	Is X going to have something?	Is X going to (do) something?
You / We / They	Are X going to be something? Are X going to be (doing) something?	Are X going to have something?	Are X going to (do) something?

Am I going to   be late?
                     Be

Am I going to   be rushing around?
                     Be (doing)

Are you going to   have time?
                        Have

Are we going to   have lunch?
                        Have

Are they going to   serve salad?
                        (Do)

Is he going to   be OK?
                        Be

Is she going to   be performing?
                        Be (doing)

Is it going to   cost money?
                        (Do)

You may have noticed that the Going To Form is structured with Be Verbs.

All three columns involve am / is / are + going to + be/have/(do).

This structure is quite long, but means the same as, **will**.

are you going to = will you   NOT: are you (doing) to

Look at the basic structures in the following chart:

Be Verb Part I: am/is/are	Subject	Be Verb Part II + Be/Have/(Do) Verb	Object
Are	you	going to be	there?
Am	I	going to be speaking	at the meeting?
Am	I	going to have	enough time?
Are	you	going to bring	a projector?

When we think about the future, we think about our future state-of-being, which is why we use a Be Verb to set up this kind of question. The second Be Verb, **going to**, only means, **will**, and therefore needs to be followed by a Full Verb.

Are you going to   **be**   something?
(There)

Are you going to   **be (doing)**   something?
(Speaking at the meeting)

Are you going to   **have**   something?
(Enough time)

Are you going to   **(do)**   something?
(Bring a projector)

Quick Practice 5: Asking Basic Questions

Fill in the following chart with sentences of your own:

Be Verb Part I: am/is/are	Subject	Be Verb Part II + Be/Have/(Do) Verb	Object
Will	you	be	home tonight?
		be (doing)	
		have	
		(do)	

Be Verb Part I: am/is/are	Subject	Be Verb Part II + Be/Have/(Do) Verb	Object
Are	you	going to be	home tonight?
		going to be (doing)	
		going to have	
		going to (do)	

Grammar Presentation 6: Short Answers

Let's start with the Will Form because it is the easiest:

Short Answers	Be	Have	(Do)
I / You / We / They / He / She / It	Yes, X will. No, X won't.	Yes, X will. No, X won't.	Yes, X will. No, X won't.

Again, all answers are the same, because the answer is understood.

Yes, I will.	(Be something)
No, I won't.	(Be something)
Yes, I will.	(Be doing something)
No, I won't.	(Be doing something)
Yes, I will.	(Have something)
No, I won't.	(Have something)
Yes, I will.	(Do something)
No, I won't.	(Do something)

Going To Short Answers	Be	Have	(Do)
I	Yes, I am. No, I am not.	Yes, I am. No, I am not.	Yes, I am. No, I am not.
He / She / It	Yes, X is. No, X is not.	Yes, X is. No, X is not.	Yes, X is. No, X is not.
You / We / They	Yes, X are. No, X are not.	Yes, X are. No, X are not.	Yes, X are. No, X are not.

Both forms can be answered with the Will Form. This just means that the person answering is thinking about a different part of the Understood English.

Question:	Answer: Understood:
Are you going to be there?	Yes, I will. (Be there)
Are you going to be there?	Yes, I am. (Going to be there)

This is not possible the other way around. Look at the following examples:

Will you be there?	Yes, I will. (Be there) NOT: Yes, I am.

Quick Practice 6: Short Answers

Circle the correct Short Answers to the following questions:

1. Are you going to do your homework?

(a) Yes, I am.
(b) Yes, I will.
(c) Yes, I have.

2. Are you going to be finishing that pizza?

(a) No, we don't
(b) No, we won't
(c) No, we aren't

3. Will you be at the concert?

(a) No, I haven't
(b) No, I won't.
(c) No, I'm not.

4. Will they have snacks?

(a) Yes, they are.
(b) Yes, they have.
(c) Yes, they will.

5. Are you going tonight?

(a) Yes, I do.
(b) Yes, I will.
(c) Yes, I am.

6. Is she singing this weekend?

(a) No, she isn't.
(b) No, she hasn't.
(c) No, she doesn't.

Grammar Presentation 7: The 5 W's and How Questions

Future Questions	Be	Have	(Do)
Who, What, Where, When, Why, How +	will (subject) be something? will (subject) be (doing) something?	will (subject) have something?	will (subject) (do) something?

Who **will I be** in 20 years?

20 years is something.

What **will I be doing** in the future?

The future is something.

Where **will I have** in my home?

My home is something.

When **will I do** it?

It is something.

Future Questions	Be	Have	(Do)
(I) Who, What, Where, When, Why, How +	am I going to be something? am I going to be (doing) something?	am I going to have something?	am I going to (do) something?
(He / She / It) Who, What, Where, When, Why, How +	is X going to be something? is X going to be (doing) something?	is X going to have something?	is X going to (do) something?
(You / We / They) Who, What, Where, When, Why, How +	are X going to be something? are X going to be (doing) something?	are X going to have something?	are X going to (do) something?

Who   am I going to be   in charge of?
Be

What   am I going to be doing   at the meeting?
Be (doing)

Where am I going to have   the presentation?
Have

When   am I going to speak   to the audience?
(Do)

Why   is he going to be   there?
Be

How   is he going to be presenting   the report?
Be (doing)

Who   is he going to have   lunch with?
Have

What   is he going to do   there?
(Do)

Where	is she going to be **Be**	in November?
When	is she going to be traveling **Be (doing)**	to Florida?
Why	is she going to have **Have**	a party?
How	is she going to do **(Do)**	that?
What	is it going to be **Be**	when it is finished?
Where	is it going to be running **Be (doing)**	the marathon?
When	is it going to have **Have**	a permanent home?
Why	is it going to operate **(Do)**	here?
How	are you going to be **Be**	on time?
Who	are you going to be working **Be (doing)**	with?
What	are you going to have **Have**	for a snack?
Where	are you going to eat **(Do)**	dinner?

What are you going to be?
What are you going to be (doing)?
What are you going to have?
What are you going to (do)?

Quick Practice 7: The 5W's and How Questions

Give true answers to the following questions, using the Going To Form:

1. Where will you **be** in one hour?

   _____.

2. What will you **be doing**?

   _____.

3. What will you **have** to eat tonight?

   _____.

4. What will you **do** this weekend?

   _____.

Fill in the following chart with questions of your own, using the Going To Form:

5W and How	Be Verb Part I: am/is/are	Subject	Be Verb Part II + Be/Have/(Do) Verb	Object
What	are	you	going to be	when you graduate?

Grammar Presentation 8: Emphatic Future Will

Notice that all of the forms are the same under the Be, Have, and (Do) Columns.

This is because the Verbs are understood.

Emphatic Will	Be	Have	(Do)
I	Yes, I will! No, I will not!	Yes, I will! No, I will not!	Yes, I will! No, I will not!
He / She / It	Yes, I will! No, I will not!	Yes, I will! No, I will not!	Yes, I will! No, I will not!
You / We / They	Yes, I will! No, I will not!	Yes, I will! No, I will not!	Yes, I will! No, I will not!

Yes, I **will**!   **be** something

Yes, I **will**!   **be doing** something

Yes, I **will**!   **have** something

Yes, I **will**!   **(do)** something

To show extra emphasis, the words are spoken separately and distinctly.

Harsh: No, I **will not!**

To sound more neutral, contractions and a softer tone are used.

More neutral: No, I **won't**.

Emphatic Will Be

To stress that we **will be** something, we simply stress the Be Verb, without using contractions.

B: You **won't** be a doctor!
A: Oh yes, I **will**!

A: You **won't be traveling** much!
B: Yes, we **will!**

To negate a statement, we place the word, **not**, after the Be Verb Combination.

Sometimes, we contract the Negative Form to make it less strong sounding.

A: I think you **will be** in America!
B: No, I **won't be** in America!

To make it sound stronger, do not use contractions.

If we do this with the Present Tense, it sounds like the speaker really does not like the idea. In the Perfect Tenses, it just sounds more emphasized. Here, it is more similar to the Present Tense and in this example it sounds like the person really does not like the idea of being in America.

Just remember that the tone you use when speaking is much more important than the actual words you use and Americans are not bothered by accents or poor grammar. What you say counts the most.

A: You **will be** in America, right?
B: No, I **will not be** in America!

A: You **will be working** as a waiter when you're 60!
B: No, I **won't**!

A: He **won't be working** very late!
B: Yes, he **will**!

Emphatic Will Have

A: You **won't have** sushi tonight!
B: Yes, I **will!**

A: Sven **will have** enough to eat next week!
B: No, he **won't!**

Emphatic Will (Do)

A: You **won't finish** the race!
B: Yes, I **will!**

A: Alicia **will fly** to St. Petersburg!
B: No, she **won't!**

Emphatic Answers for the Going To Form:

Emphatic Going To	Be	Have	(Do)
I	Yes, I am! No, I am not!	Yes, I am! No, I am not!	Yes, I am! No, I am not!
He / She / It	Yes, X is! No, X is not!	Yes, X is! No, X is not!	Yes, X is! No, X is not!
You / We / They	Yes, X are! No, X are not!	Yes, X are! No, X are not!	Yes, X are! No, X are not!

Notice that all of the forms are the same under the Be, Have, and (Do) Columns. This is because the Verbs are understood.

Yes, I **am going to**   **be** something

Yes, I **am going to**   **be doing** something

Yes, I **am going to**   **have** something
Yes, I **am going to**   **(do)** something

To show extra emphasis, the words are spoken separately and distinctly.

Harsh: No, I **am not!**

To sound more neutral, contractions and a softer tone are used.

More neutral: No, **I'm not.**

Emphatic Going To Be

To stress that we **are going to be** something, we simply stress the Be Verb, without using Contractions.

B: You **are not going to be** a doctor!
A: Oh yes, I **am!**

A: You **are not going to be traveling** much!
B: Yes, we **are!**

To negate a statement, we place the word, **not**, after the Be Verb Combination.

Sometimes, we contract the Negative to make it less strong sounding.

A: I think you **are going to be** in America!
B: **I'm not going to be** in America!

To make it sound stronger, do not use contractions.

If we do this with the Present Tense, it sounds like the speaker really does not like the idea. In the Perfect Tenses, it just sounds more emphasized.

Here, it is more similar to the Present Tense and in this example it sounds like the person really does not like the idea of being in America.

But, like everything, the tone dictates the meaning more than the actual words.

A: You **are going to be** in America, right?
B: No, I **am not going to be** in America!

Emphatic Going To Have

A: You **aren't going to have** sushi tonight!
B: Yes, I **am!**

A: Sven **is going to have** enough to eat next week!
B: No, he **isn't!**

Emphatic Going To (Do)

A: You **aren't going to finish** the race!
B: Yes, I **am!**

A: Alicia **is going to fly** to St. Petersburg!
B: No, she **isn't!**

Quick Practice 8: Emphatic Future

Respond to the following mean-hearted statements with Emphatic Short Answers, using the Will Form:

1. You will be a failure!

    _____!

2. You will be working forever!

    _____!

3. You will have no luck!

    _____!

4. You will go crazy!

    _____!

5. You will never find love!

    _____!

6. You will go to jail!

    _____!

Now do the same thing in the Going To Form:

7. You are not going to be a success!

    _____!

8. You are not going to be smiling!

    _____!

9. You are not going to have fun!

    _____!

10. You are not going to succeed!

    _____!

11. People are not going to like you!

    _____!

12. Your life is not going to be good!

    _____!

Review Your Knowledge:

We have three ways to talk about the future. You can use any of these forms in most situations:

I	**will open** **(Do)**	**a B&B soon.**
I	**am going to open** **(Do)**	**a B&B soon.**
I	**am opening** **(Do)**	**a B&B soon.**

One main difference is when we are speaking and making spontaneous decisions. In this case, we use the shorter Will Form:

A: Oops! I spilled my drink!
B: Oh, I will get you a new one.

The Will Form can have Contractions:

I'll be in New York tomorrow.

The Going To Form does not have Contractions, but you can still contract the Subject:

I'm going to be in New York tomorrow.

For the Will Form, Positive and Negative Short Answers are the same for all Subjects:

Yes, I will.

No, I won't.

Emphatic Answers are the same for all Subjects in the Will Form:

Yes, I will!

No, I will not!

Will Be Something
Will Be (Doing) Something
Will Have Something
Will (Do) Something

Going To Be Something
Going To Be (Doing) Something
Going To Have Something
Going To (Do) Something

Exercises for Reinforcing Grammar

Show the Future Simple and Progressive Forms for the Will Form:

Future	Be	Have	(Do)
I / You / We / They / He / She / It	_____ _____	_____	_____

Show the Future Simple and Progressive Forms for the Going To Form:

Future	Be	Have	(Do)
I	_____ _____	_____	_____
He / She / It	_____ _____	_____	_____
You / We / They	_____ _____	_____	_____

Show the Future Contraction Forms for the Will Form:

Future	Be	Have	(Do)
I	_____	_____	_____
You	_____	_____	_____
We	_____	_____	_____
They	_____	_____	_____
He	_____	_____	_____
She	_____	_____	_____
It	_____	_____	_____

Show the Basic Question Forms for the Will Form:

Future	Be	Have	(Do)
I / You / We / They / He / She / It	_____ _____	_____	_____

Show the Basic Question Forms for the Going To Form:

Future	Be	Have	(Do)
I	_____ _____	_____	_____
He / She / It	_____ _____	_____	_____
You / We / They	_____ _____	_____	_____

Answer the 5W Questions with the Will Form:

1. Who will you be for Halloween?

   I don't know _____.

2. What will you be dressing up as for Halloween?

   I don't know _____.

3. What will he have for dinner?

   I don't know _____.

4. Who will they go to the dance with?

   I don't know _____.

5.   Where will we be two years from now?

      I don't know _____.

6.   When will she go to Belgium?

      I don't know _____.

7.   Why will they stop selling that product?

      I don't know _____.

8.   How will they have enough chairs?

      I don't know _____.

Now answer the same 5W Questions with the Going to Form:

9.   Who are you going to be for Halloween?

      I don't know _____.

10.   What are you going to be dressing up as for Halloween?

      I don't know _____.

11.   What is he going to have for dinner?

      I don't know _____.

12.   Who are they going to go to the dance with?

      I don't know _____.

13.   Where are we going to be two years from now?

      I don't know _____.

14.   When is she going to go to Belgium?

      I don't know _____.

15. Why are they going to stop selling that product?

I don't know _____.

16. How are they going to have enough chairs?

I don't know _____.

Look Again! This Is What We Have Learned!

The Will Form:

Future Will	Be	Have	(Do)
	Future Simple or Future Progressive	Future Simple	Future Simple
Future Simple Future Progressive	X will be something. X will be (doing) something.	X will have something. ---	X will (do) something. ---
Question Form Emphatic Form	Will X be something? Yes, X will! No, X will not!	Will X have something? Yes, X will! No, X will not!	Will X (do) something? Yes, X will! No, X will not!

The Going To Form:

Future Going To	Be	Have	(Do)
	Future Simple or Future Progressive	Future Simple	Future Simple
(I) Future Simple Future Progressive Question Form Emphatic Form	I am going to be something. I am going to be (doing) something. Am I going to be something? Yes, I am! No, I am not!	I am going to have something. --- Am I going to have something? Yes, I am! No, I am not!	I am going to (do) something. --- Am I going to (do) something? Yes, I am! No, I am not!
(He / She / It) Future Simple Future Progressive Question Form Emphatic Form	X is going to be something. X is going to be (doing) something. Is X going to be something? Yes, X is! No, X is not!	X is going to have something. --- Is X going to have something? Yes, X is! No, X is not!	X is going to (do) something. --- Is X going to (do) something? Yes, X is! No, X is not!
(You / We / They) Future Simple Future Progressive Question Form Emphatic Form	X are going to be something. X are going to be (doing) something. Are X going to be something? Yes, X are! No, X are not!	X are going to have something. --- Are X going to have something? Yes, X are! No, X are not!	X are going to (do) something. --- Are X going to (do) something? Yes, X are! No, X are not!

Crazy Culture Tip

Activate Student's Knowledge: What do you know about laws in the US? Do you have funny laws in your country? Read the following text for Comprehension:

America is the land of laws.

Look at some of the crazy things that are illegal (or legal) in the United States:

Arkansas: A man can only beat his wife once a month.

Alabama: It is illegal to play Solitaire on Sundays.

Arizona: It is illegal to refuse someone a glass of water.

California: It is illegal to eat an orange in the bathtub.

Colorado: It is illegal to borrow your neighbor's vacuum cleaner in Denver.

Florida: It is illegal to dream about a neighbor's wife or cow.

Georgia: If they are walking to school together, girls have to offer to carry boy's books.

Hawaii: It is illegal to be in public wearing swimming shorts and you can be fined for not owning a boat.

Indiana: It is illegal to take a bath in winter.

Minnesota: It is illegal to sleep naked.

Mississippi: It is illegal to shave without a Shaving Permit.

Oklahoma: It is illegal to take a bite of someone else's hamburger.

Oregon: It is illegal to eat ice-cream on Sundays.

Texas: It is illegal to go barefoot unless you have a permit.

Virginia: It is illegal to have sex unless you are married.

Washington: Lollipops are illegal.

Wyoming: It is illegal for a man to tickle a woman.

Washington DC: People do not have the same right to vote as other Americans.

Source: www.informationcentral0.tripod.com

Fun with Five

Character:	Written / Spoken:
5th	Fifth
5x	Five times
5	Five
55	Fifty-five
555	Five hundred fifty-five
555 1/5	Five hundred fifty-five and one fifth
$5.00	Five dollars
$5.55	Five dollars **and** fifty-five cent**s**
$555.00	Five hundred fifty-five dollar**s**
$555.55	Five hundred fifty-five dollar**s and** fifty-five cent**s**
V	Roman numeral five
LV	Roman numeral fifty-five

Look up the following words, which all have something to do with the word five, and see what you learn:

Quintuplets-   Pentagon-

What do these phrases mean? Do you have words for these things in your language?

High five-   Hang five-

Take five-   Five o'clock shadow-

Answer Key

Quick Practice 1: The Future Tense   **Page   14**

1.   A: Where will you go to college*?
      B: I **am going to** go to UCLA. I got accepted last month!
2.   A: Where will you go to college?
      B: I'm not sure. I think I **will** spend a year at community college.
3.   A: Oops! I dropped my cell phone!
      B: Don't worry; I **will** get that for you.
4.   A: What are you doing this weekend?
      B: I don't know. I think I **will** have a BBQ.
5.   A: What are you doing this weekend?
      B: I **am going to** have a BBQ. We planned it last week.

Future	Be	Have	(Do)
Future Simple	**will be** **going to be**	**will have** **going to have**	**will (do)** **going to (do)**
Future Progressive	**will be (doing)** **going to be (doing)**		

Future Contractions	Be	Have	(Do)
I	**I'll be** I'll not be* **I won't be**	**I'll have** I'll not have* **I won't have**	**I'll (do)** I'll not (do)* **I won't (do)**
He	**He'll be** He'll not be* **He won't be**	**He'll have** He'll not have* **He won't have**	**He'll (do)** He'll not (do)* **He won't (do)**
She	**She'll be** She'll not be* **She won't be**	**She'll have** She'll not have* **She won't have**	**She'll (do)** She'll not (do)* **She won't (do)**
It	**It'll be** It'll not be* **It won't be**	**It'll have** It'll not have* **It won't have**	**It'll (do)** It'll not (do)* **It won't (do)**
You	**You'll be** You'll not be* **You won't be**	**You'll have** You'll not have* **You won't have**	**You'll (do)** You'll not (do)* **You won't (do)**

We	We'll be	We'll have	We'll (do)
	We'll not be* **We won't be**	We'll not have* **We won't have**	We'll not (do)* **We won't (do)**
They	**They'll be**	**They'll have**	**They'll (do)**
	They'll not be* **They won't be**	They'll not have* **They won't have**	They'll not (do)* **They won't (do)**

Quick Practice 2: Positive and Negative Contractions Page   16

Please check your answers with your teacher.

Quick Practice 3: Basic Building Blocks   Page   20

Please check your answers with your teacher.

Quick Practice 4: Present Tense for the Future   Page   22

Please check your answers with your teacher.

Quick Practice 5: Asking Basic Questions   Page   26

Please check your answers with your teacher.

Quick Practice 6: Short Answers   Page   28

1. Are you going to do your homework?

(a) Yes, I am.
(b) Yes, I will.
(c) Yes, I have.

3. Will you be at the concert?
(a) No, I haven't
(b) No, I won't.
(c) No, I'm not.

5. Are you going tonight?

(a) Yes, I do.
(b) Yes, I will.
(c) Yes, I am.

2. Are you going to be finishing that pizza?
(a) No, we don't
(b) No, we won't
(c) No, we aren't

4. Will they have snacks?
(a) Yes, they are.
(b) Yes, they have.
(c) Yes, they will.

6. Is she singing this weekend?
(a) No, she isn't.
(b) No, she hasn't.
(c) No, she doesn't.

Quick Practice 7: The 5W's and How Questions   Page   32

1.	(Be)	Where will you be in one hour?	I will be...
2.	(Be)	What will you be doing?	I will be...
3.	(Have)	What will you have to eat tonight?	I will have...
4.	(Do)	What will you do this weekend?	I will...

Quick Practice 8: Emphatic Future   Page   37

1.	You will be a failure!	No, I won't!
2.	You will be working forever!	No, I won't!
3.	You will have no luck!	Yes, I will!
4.	You will go crazy!	No, you won't!
5.	You will never find love!	Yes, I will!
6.	You will go to jail!	No, I won't!
7.	You are not going to be a success!	Yes, I am!
8.	You are not going to be smiling!	Yes, I am!
9.	You are not going to have fun!	Yes, I am!
10.	You are not going to succeed!	Yes, I am!
11.	People are not going to like you!	Yes, they are!
12.	Your life is not going to be good!	Yes, it is!

Exercises for Reinforcing Grammar   Page   39

Future Tense Will Positive	Be	Have	(Do)
I / You / We / They / He / She / It	will be something will be (doing) something	will have something	will (do) something

Future Tense Will Negative	Be	Have	(Do)
I / You / We / They / He / She / It	will not be something will not be (doing)	will not have something	will not (do) something

Future Tense Going To Positive	Be	Have	(Do)
I	am going to be something am going to be (doing) something	am going to have something	am going to (do) something
He / She / It	is going to be something is going to be	is going to have something	is going to (do) something

	(doing) something		
You / We / They	are going to be something are going to be (doing) something	are going to have something	are going to (do) something

Future Tense Going To Negative	Be	Have	(Do)
I	am not going to be something am not going to be (doing) something	am not going to have something	am not going to (do) something
He / She / It	is not going to be something is not going to be (doing) something	is not going to have something	is not going to (do) something
You / We / They	are not going to be something are not going to be (doing) something	are not going to have something	are not going to (do) something

Future Contractions	Be	Have	(Do)
I	I'll be I'll not be* I won't be	I'll have I'll not have* I won't have	I'll (do) I'll not (do)* I won't (do)
He	He'll be He'll not be* He won't be	He'll have He'll not have* He won't have	He'll (do) He'll not (do)* He won't (do)
She	She'll be	She'll have	She'll (do)

	She'll not be* **She won't be**	She'll not have* **She won't have**	She'll not (do)* **She won't (do)**
It	**It'll be** It'll not be* **It won't be**	**It'll have** It'll not have* **It won't have**	**It'll (do)** It'll not (do)* **It won't (do)**
You	**You'll be** You'll not be* **You won't be**	**You'll have** You'll not have* **You won't have**	**You'll (do)** You'll not (do)* **You won't (do)**
We	**We'll be** We'll not be* **We won't be**	**We'll have** We'll not have* **We won't have**	**We'll (do)** We'll not (do)* **We won't (do)**
They	**They'll be** They'll not be* **They won't be**	**They'll have** They'll not have* **They won't have**	**They'll (do)** They'll not (do)* **They won't (do)**

Will Questions	Be	Have	(Do)
I / You / We / They / He / She / It	**Will X be something?** **Will X be (doing) something?**	**Will X have something?**	**Will X (do) something?**

Going To Questions	Be	Have	(Do)
I	**Am I going to be something?** **Am I going to be (doing) something?**	**Am I going to have something?**	**Am I going to (do) something?**
He / She / It	**Is X going to be something?** **Is X going to be (doing) something?**	**Is X going to have something?**	**Is X going to (do) something?**
You / We / They	**Are X going to be something?**	**Are X going to have something?**	**Are X going to (do) something?**

	Are X going to be (doing) something?		

1.   Who will you be for Halloween?
I don't know who I will be for Halloween.
2.   What will you be dressing up as for Halloween?
I don't know what I will be dressing up as for Halloween.
3.   What will he have for dinner?
I don't know what he will have for dinner.
4.   Who will they go to the dance with?
I don't know who they will go to the dance with.
5.   Where will we be two years from now?
I don't know where we will be two years from now.
6.   When will she go to Belgium?
I don't know when she will go to Belgium.
7.   Why will they stop selling that product?
I don't know why they will stop selling that product.
8.   How will they have enough chairs?
I don't know how they will have enough chairs.
9.   Who are you going to be for Halloween?
I don't know who I am going to be for Halloween.
10.   What are you going to be dressing up as for Halloween?
I don't know what I am going to be dressing up as for Halloween.
11.   What is he going to have for dinner?
I don't know what he is going to have for dinner.
12.   Who are they going to go to the dance with?
I don't know who they are going to go to the dance with.
13.   Where are we going to be two years from now?
I don't know where we are going to be two years from now.
14.   When is she going to go to Belgium?
I don't know when she is going to go to Belgium.
15.   Why are they going to stop selling that product?
I don't know why they are going to stop selling that product.
16.   How are they going to have enough chairs?
I don't know how they are going to have enough chairs.

Congratulations!

You made it through the Be/Have/(Do) Grammar Matrix Single Lesson Five: The Future Tenses!

Ready for more?

Check out all 15 books in this series. Single Lesson One – Single Lesson Six cover grammar and Single Lesson Seven – Single Lesson Fourteen cover Verbs, and Nouns, and Single Lesson: The Appendices covers Fun and Interesting Facts, Tables, and other Grammar Structures.

Coming Soon: How to Think in English: Be Something! Have Something! Do Something! Book Three: The Sayings

Learn 500 Idioms, Sayings, and English Proverbs. You will be speaking like a native in no time!

On The Go?

Check us out at www.BeHaveDo.com!

Check out my Facebook Fan Page: John C Lipes

Follow These Lessons with Video Tutorials on our YouTube Channel: John C Lipes

Words to Live By

The following is a poem that was written by Max Ehrmann in Terre Haute, Indiana in the early 1900's.

Much controversy surrounds the copyrights of this beautiful work.

Look in the Internet to see what you can find out about this poem.

Desiderata

Go placidly amid the noise and haste,
And remember what peace there may be in silence.

As far as possible, without surrender,
Be on Good terms with all persons.
Speak your truth quietly and clearly;
And listen to others, even the dull and ignorant;
They too have their story.

Avoid loud and aggressive persons;
They are vexations to the spirit.
If you compare yourself with others,
You may become vain and bitter;
For always there will be greater
And lesser persons than yourself.

Enjoy your achievements as well as your plans.
Keep interested in your own career, however humble;
It is a real possession in the changing fortunes of
time.
Exercise caution in your business affairs;
For the world is full of trickery.

But let this not blind you to what virtue there is;
Many persons strive for high ideals;
And everywhere life is full of heroism.

Be yourself, especially, do not feign affection.
Neither be cynical about love for in the
face of all aridity and disenchantment
It is perennial as the grass.

Take kindly the counsel of the years,
Gracefully surrendering the things of youth.
Nurture strength of spirit to shield you in
sudden misfortune. But do not distress yourself
with imaginings. Many fears are born of fatigue
and loneliness. Beyond a wholesome discipline,
Be gentle with yourself.

You are a child of the universe,
No less than the trees and the stars;
You have a right to be here.
And whether or not it is clear to you,
No doubt the universe is unfolding as it should.

Therefore be at peace with God,
Whatever you conceive him to be,
And whatever your labors and aspirations,
In the noisy confusion of live, keep peace with your
soul.

With all its shams, drudgery,
And broken dreams,
It is still a beautiful world.

Strive to be Happy.

How to Think in English: Be Something! Have Something! Do Something!
Book One and Book Two in Full Color

Learn English Grammar and Vocabulary in One Book with Answer Key!

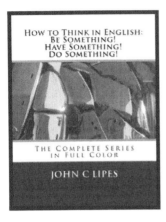

8.5" x 11" (21.59 x 27.94 cm)

Saves Time!

Full Color on White paper
490 pages
ISBN-13: 978-1480092358
ISBN-10: 1480092355

This Full Color Complete How to Think in English Series covers all aspects of the language from a-z. Get the Whole Series in One Volume! Learn how to speak and think in English sentence structures with the Be/Have/(Do) Grammar Matrix. A new and easy way to learn Grammar for all learners of English and ESL.

Be Something!

Have Something!

Do Something!

www.BeHaveDo.com

www.bedandbay.com

www.amazon.com/author/johnclipes

Facebook: John C Lipes

How to Think in English: Be Something! Have Something! Do Something!
Book One: The Tenses

Learn the English Grammar Tenses with Answer Key!

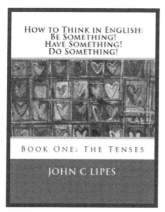

8.5" x 11" (21.59 x 27.94 cm)

Saves Time!

Full Color on White paper
266 pages
ISBN-13: 978-1480085923
ISBN-10: 1480085928

Covers Material from Single Lessons One – Six. This new way to learn English will make learning Grammar easy. Book One: The Tenses. Book Two: Actions and Things.

Look for the entire series of Be/Have/(Do) Methodology Books by John C Lipes.

Be Something!

Have Something!

Do Something!

www.BeHaveDo.com

www.bedandbay.com

www.amazon.com/author/johnclipes

Facebook: John C Lipes

How to Think in English: Be Something! Have Something! Do Something!
Book Two: Actions and Things

Learn How to Build Vocabulary with Verbs and Nouns with Answer Key!

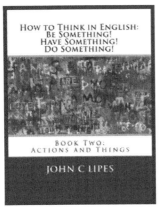

8.5" x 11" (21.59 x 27.94 cm)

Saves Time!

Full Color on White paper
287 pages
ISBN-13: 978-1480086203
ISBN-10: 1480086207

Covers Material from Single Lessons Seven – Thirteen. Do you want to learn how to speak and understand English? Do you hate grammar? Wait until you see my new way to learn English.

How to Think in English: Be Something! Have Something! Do Something! was inspired by my students!

Be Something!

Have Something!

Do Something!

www.BeHaveDo.com

www.bedandbay.com

www.amazon.com/author/johnclipes

Facebook: John C Lipes

How to Think in English: Be Something! Have Something! Do Something!

Book One and Book Two in Black and White

Learn English Grammar and Vocabulary in One Book with Answer Key!

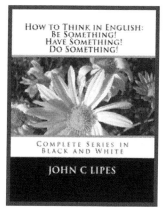

8.5" x 11" (21.59 x 27.94 cm)

Saves Money!

Black & White on White paper
490 pages
ISBN-13: 978-1480097858
ISBN-10: 1480097853

This is the Black and White Version of the Complete Be/Have/(Do) Grammar Matrix Series.

A must for all ESL students or anyone who wants to learn how to speak and think in English. This new method makes learning fun and easy by dividing the language into three areas.

Be Something!

Have Something!

Do Something!

www.BeHaveDo.com

www.bedandbay.com

www.amazon.com/author/johnclipes

Facebook: John C Lipes

How to Think in English: Be Something! Have Something! Do Something!

Book One: The Tenses

Learn the English Grammar Tenses with Answer Key!

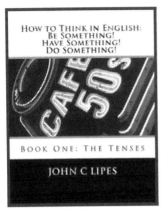

8.5" x 11" (21.59 x 27.94 cm)

Saves Money!

Black & White on White paper

266 pages

ISBN-13: 978-1480093058

ISBN-10: 148009305X

This is the Black and White Version, designed to save you money and help you learn English in a new and fun way.!

Covers Material from Single Lessons One – Six. Learn how to speak and think in English grammatical structures in a new and easy way called the Be/Have/(Do) Grammar Matrix for learning English!

Be Something!

Have Something!

Do Something!

www.BeHaveDo.com

www.bedandbay.com

www.amazon.com/author/johnclipes

Facebook: John C Lipes

How to Think in English: Be Something! Have Something! Do Something!   Book Two: Actions and Things

Learn How to Build Vocabulary with Verbs and Nouns with Answer Key!

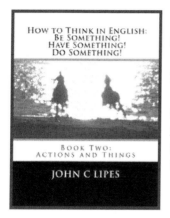

8.5" x 11" (21.59 x 27.94 cm)

Saves Money!

Black & White on White paper
287 pages
ISBN-13: 978-1480093362
ISBN-10: 148009336X

This is the Black and White Version of Book Two: Actions and Things in the Be/Have/(Do) Grammar Matrix Series, which was designed to save you money and teach you English grammar in a brand new way that is fun and easy.

For all ESL students or anyone who wants to learn how to speak and think in English. Covers Material from Single Lessons Seven – Thirteen.

Be Something!

Have Something!

Do Something!

www.BeHaveDo.com

www.bedandbay.com

www.amazon.com/author/johnclipes

Facebook: John C Lipes

Printed in Great Britain
by Amazon.co.uk, Ltd.,
Marston Gate.